PREFACE

I stumbled across Simon's images for 40 whilst idly surfing the net. There the  green waves on a summer beach. I was captivated by them from the start. T   about the man who walked into the desert in these pictures, and somehow so familiar- like a lost relative not seen since childhood. The power of the simple lines drew me back to that place, and for that I am grateful.

Pretty soon, we decided to use the images as part of a dramatic worship offering, and I began to write the words in this book as a sort of script. You, however, can use them as you will. You might use them alone, or in a group. You might carry the book into your own place of wilderness, real or metaphorical. You might laugh and joke with us, or you may cry. You may already be a person of faith who is looking for a new understanding of a familiar story, or you may be searching out a new spiritual path.

 My prayer for you all is that as you turn the pages of this book, you meet a man called Jesus.

Chris Goan
Dunoon, Scotland
February 2007

In a room scented by the smell of sawn timber, a man hears a voice in his inner ear calling him

it is time -
your time, and mine

enough of the mending and making and shaping of wood

time to put aside the tools

the sharp nails...
can wait.

While the village still slept, he set his face to the low morning light and followed this beautiful voice

calling him
leading him
drawing him

into wilderness.

He did not look back to the comforts of home, but walked on...

into the desert - the place of suffering and desolation, where each rock hid its own danger
every stone could strike at the heel

he walked onwards
alone.

As he walked he left something of himself behind

the skin of civilisation was being burnt away by the hot sun

driven away by the wild animals

but in the rhythm of every step was the music of this voice - singing to his soul

it's your time... and mine.

After a time, the desert seemed so big, and he -
so small

a panic rose in him
it clutched him like a hand at his throat

    Who am I?
    What am I?
    What terrible road lies before me?
    Father, my body is weak
    I am a drop of water
    On a rock
    Under the hot desert sun
    Soon I will be gone

still he walked
still he followed
that voice.

Dust devils plucked specks from the sand and spat them at his face

walk on my son
this is your time... and mine.

He followed the voice into dark canyons carved by raging streams now long dry

and he was grateful to leave behind the dark places

to climb towards light.

And from a high place he watched in wonder as the sun sank into desert sea

he watched as it stained the sand like wine spreading on a table

like blood.

As evening fell he looked for a place to rest

the dry desert skies sucked back the warmth from the ground as he lay down his head

and the night creatures were set loose
hungry and wild.

A weak morning light filtered into the ravine where he slept and he woke

that restlessness was there still
gnawing at him
calling him on

now is your time... and mine
now is your time... and mine.

Find me O my father
Make me
Take me back to you
My throat is cracked
But thirst is more
For you
My stomach craves
A food that feeds only this –
My soul

So I walk
Desperate
Close to falling
Stumbling...

To you.

At his lowest point a blessing fell at his feet

a sound brought him to some rocks, and he peered over into the shade and saw foxes at play

the cubs left their lair and tripped over each other, nibbling ears and licking fur, oblivious to his presence, at one with all things

the pure joy of the moment found its way into the very centre of him
it lit up his soul

desert became paradise

Father came to son.

The joy in his heart could not stay still
it found its way to his feet
and made a dance

what a dance!

his sandals beat the dust
and his clothes cracked the air about him.

He danced down valleys and over stream beds

he danced the day long...

    A dance for the hungry and thirsty
    A dance for the broken and hurting
    A dance for the widows and the fatherless children
    A dance for the lonely and the betrayed
    A dance for the poor in spirit
           and those captive to the night
    A dance for those downcast and robbed of hope
    A dance for the dying and those left in grief
    A dance for those who suffer and need relief
    A dance of grace, and love, and mercy
    A *freedom* dance...
    For all mankind

and as he danced, he drove away those black birds of death and hate and war,
and profiteering, and slavery -
evil took to flight

this day belonged to the dancer -
and the dance.

Exhausted now

burned up

the responsibilities of this journey
the burdens to carry on the way
the *foolishness* of the dance

and his dreams lay like bleached bones at his feet.

The terrible black birds drew near again

drawn to the sweet smell of carrion
blown in on the breeze.

That night, he stood alone before the moon
listening again for the voice
straining for its music

his face shone with the reflected light
sun to moon
moon to face
and he started to hope again

    Now is your time my son
    In you are *my* hopes - my dreams
    In you is everything I am
    In you is all my love, all my mercy, all my grace

    Yes now is your time... and mine.

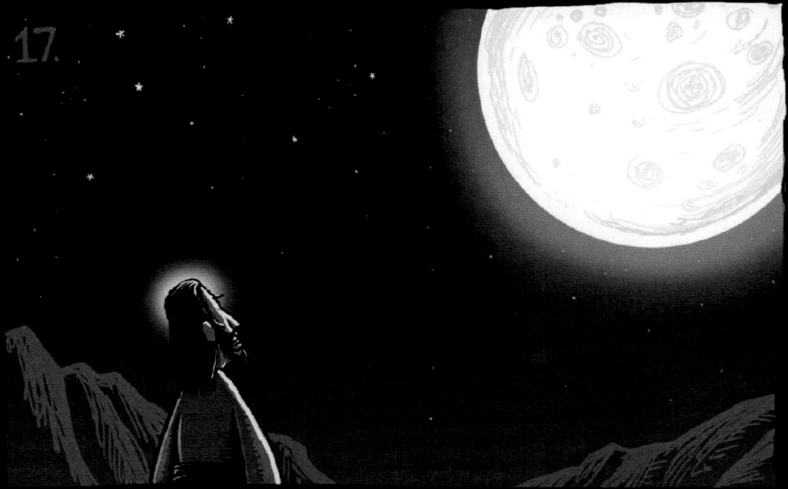
17.

Huge drops pound at the dust
the rain makes the air as sweet as a rich ripe grape
the dust turns to dirt, and the dirt becomes soil

and the water finds it way into cracks in the parched ground

seeking out dry steam beds

searching out seeds long left behind
opening again those forgotten kernels of truth and life
letting them become again what they once were

rain falling on his head
running down his beard

anointing
baptising

bathing and soothing.

And from the depths of his learning, singing in his heart, come the words of
the poet-prophet Isaiah

> The poor and needy search for water but find none
> Their tongues are parched and dry
> But *I* am there to be found. I do not forget
> I will burst forth rivers from barren hills
> Send fountains from valleys
> I'll turn sun scorched desert into a still lake
> And water the waste lands with cool streams
>
> Fix your eyes on my servant
> in whom I am well pleased.

And in the dark earth, a flower found itself again, and pushed out into the daylight

he looked upon this new wonder, held in the spell of such delicate beauty

he dreamed of a new beginning
a new springtime

is it *now* father?
is now our time?

It seemed for a while that he was no longer alien in this place

the earth had remembered him.

He walked on into days
still drawn by the voice - now right here
then distant

one moment closer than his own heartbeat,
then just a distant whisper on the desert wind

now is your time my son
and through you, I will make all things new...

Time lost meaning

hours passed and faded into days
he walked half in this world, and half in another

a sharp stone poked him into reality and he picked it up

a stone to make men stumble
and a rock to make them fall.

Even here there were distractions - temptations

like a deadly fruit that promised a relief from cravings, but brought instead sickness, and death.

Here too was cruelty

the desert reached out and tore at him

thorns scarred his body – ripping into his flesh
all too soon to become
his crown.

Each day bore down -
horizons liquid in the heat

but he does not stop

walking, walking, walking...

listening.

He was a man, and men need rest

so evil saw its chance

it stalked him
ready to strike.

But from the man arose a prayer:

You are my shepherd
You bring me to lie in the lush green pasture
And find me the coolest pools to drink from
You guide me along paths of righteousness
And restore my troubled soul
Even when my way goes through the valley of the dead
I fear no evil
For you walk with me.

You serve me the finest food
Right before the enemy
You lift my broken head
And pour on me your blessing
And your shepherds crook keeps me safe
Your beauty and love chase after me all my life
And soon, I'll come home
For ever.

So broken, and exhausted - he looked for a place to rest

Hide me O my father
Be my safe place
Be my shelter

Cover me from the heat of this day.

A cave welcomed him
and held him in its hollows

shrouding him from the weary walk

it became for him the whole world
for a while.

So, empty

drained

poured out to the point
of death

entombed within this body
death draws close
and finds welcome.

The night came in unnoticed
but in his dream the man still heard
the voice

now my son, now is your time
your time
and mine.

Suddenly he was not alone
across the desert strides a stranger

there is something friendly and familiar about him-
he is cool and clean and his voice is like butter

but beneath this fine exterior there is something more
old - older than mankind
in his eyes there are the depths of darkness and destruction
epidemics rage there

in the corner of his gaze savage creatures rip and claw at one another

he flicks a glance and arrows fly
cannons fire and flame

and in the pool of his vision men and women objectify each other, and lust for power and
money and sex

rivers flow toxic in his tears

now he has a new mission...

The two men walk out into the sun
 so begins the first attack

Son of God - what a fool you are to suffer such hunger! You hold the power to snuff out the sun,
but you go hungry? Perhaps you are not so strong after all?

If you were - you could turn these very stones to bread, and we could share sandwiches for
breakfast!

we need so much more
than bread

I am the bread of life
and I come to feed souls.

With flashing eyes the stranger turns and in a blink they stand high on the temple walls looking far down on the courtyard

and then - the second attack.

I don't think you are him at all! Look at you - standing there all weak at the knees!
If you were precious to your father, you could throw yourself from this place and the angels would catch in mid-air and float you softly to the stone floors below.

Go on...DO it.
SHOW me!

I must....not...test...my father.

(Now is your time my precious son - and mine.)

With a howl of disgust the stranger turned back again and took the man to the high places overlooking a huge city

so began the third attack.

LOOK you fool - all this could be yours! You cower in the desert but the whole world is at MY feet!

I can give you anything you could ever want -
money, power, servants, fame, influence - SIGNIFICANCE!
Are these things not necessary to complete this mission of yours?

Why not do things in style?
Why grovel in the dirt when you can live like a king?

All I would ask is this - do it my way
Listen to ME...

ENOUGH!
I serve only one master

the spirit of my sovereign Lord is on me
he has sent me to the poor and the weak with good news

he has told me that it is time to heal the broken hearted
he shouts FREEDOM to all captives,
and breaks the chains of those you have bound!

now is the time of my Father's grace
and the destruction of your plans!

and the stranger

was gone.

Exhausted - battle done
the man fell back into the dust

the desert once again pulled at his bones
sucking the moisture from his flesh

but this was not the end

it was the beginning.

So the journey continued.
back into the world of men...

To all the homes and houses
And broken down old shacks
To the priests and to the soldiers
To the slaves and the fat cats
To the athletes and the cripples
To the beggar and his King
To the broken and the dying
And those who have no song to sing

Into the place of children's squabbles
And where folk gossip in the town square
Hear the singing from the synagogue
Calling the town to prayer

To all this living and this loving -
This fecundity of life

Now it is your time my friends

And mine.

NOTES ON WILDERNESS:

The story of Jesus in the desert meets us in many different ways. It is an amazing account of God taking on the feeble form of a created being and experiencing the utter humility of unprotected isolation in barren wilderness. This story has also become our story- part of the glorious history of our family of faith, celebrated each year in the season of Lent. But it is also the very human story of one man carrying the huge burden of his calling, seeking strength to come to terms with the task that lay before him, and refusing to accept the short cuts and compromises offered by the enemy.

The word wilderness conjures up powerful biblical images. Throughout the history of the Bible, it is always there in the background- a desolate and challenging backdrop. It symbolises solitude, desolation, and separation from the security of family and community. The Bible tells us of leaders driven into wilderness to restore their vision, to be alone with the Almighty, and to prepare them for the things ahead. Perhaps you have had your own times of wilderness- of wandering in a hostile landscape, looking for safety and a sure path- alone and at times afraid. If so, we hope that this book might be a small help as you continue in your own journey.

Someone told me once that the word humble derives from the Latin word Humus, meaning 'soil', or 'ground'. From the ground, we were formed- to this ground, we all return one day. Knowledge of our fragility and our oh-so-short short stay within these ancient landscapes perhaps brings the ultimate humility. The mountains and hills are so big, and we are so small. The seas go on for ever. The deserts could swallow us all and remain unconcerned and unmoved. In this place of vulnerability, away from the illusion safety given by our modern lifestyles, perhaps we come to understand our place in the world with so much more clarity. Or at least that has been my experience.

I easily hold to a romantic idea of wild places. My understanding is forged by televisual abstracted images. It lacks subjectivity. For many however, wilderness is a place of suffering, a place of toil and of survival against the odds. I am usually a grateful day tripper (or perhaps a weekend back backer), heading home satisfied for a warm bath and a washing machine, so only speak about these things as a reader of other peoples stories. But for those who tread the highest mountains, or trace rivers into dark Jungle, or walk for hours in order to find food and water for themselves and their families- wilderness is not a postcard. It is hardship and toil, fear and danger, reducing the strongest and most powerful man to a mere grain of sand on an ocean floor.

God said that his strength is made perfect in our weakness. In our surrender of power and control, we find his strength. Perhaps wilderness is the ultimate reminder of this...

I have known another kind of wilderness too- a wilderness of spirit, when a terrible loneliness and emptiness seemed to define my days. I looked for safety, security, but all I found was the cold shelter of a mountain howf, a rock shelter. I cried out to God, but he seemed not to hear me.

What might take us to these places? Why do we go there? I have met many who seem to have fallen there by accident. Events have overtaken them, such as bereavement, or loss of job, livelihood and purpose. Some others were carried into the wilderness by parents who abandoned them in the hills amongst the wild animals, and they have spent a lifetime trying to find the trail home. Some preachers tell us that we may be there because of bad navigation. By wilful neglect of the rules God gave us for living together in the Promised Land. Maybe by corrupt business, or lust for power, money or sex. We become outcasts, unworthy, unclean- sent out by our communities to wander as penance, longing for redemption. I spent years thinking that my sin had driven God away from me. I could never be acceptable, never be good enough, and so I stayed in the wild places, alone.

Many of us, like Job, cast about looking for meaning in desolation, endlessly trying to understand how we entered the wilderness, and what it is for. We ask "Where am I?" "Who am I?" "Why are these things happening to me?" but seem to find no answers. God is so distant, prayers seem futile. We are told to "seek the Lord while he may be found"- could it be that He has gone off to another place and left us, abandoned and alone?

For a while, the wilderness became my home. It was familiar, and in a strange way, asked less of me than other warm and cultivated places. Anyway, I did not know where these other places were, and feared their scrutiny, and certain rejection. So like Elijah, I hid from my enemies in the wild places, angry with God and man- even as His ravens sought me out with food. I stayed there, and licked my wounds.

But wilderness can also be a place of blessing. A place from which all things begin, right before the fulfilment of the promises of God. It was in that place of solitude that God began to reveal to me who I was, and could be.

I follow in a fine tradition. The Bible is full of stories of people in wilderness...

• Abraham left home and family and set out into the wilderness. It was the only way to become the great man that God planned him to be.
• **Joseph**, the powerful leader began his journey into Egypt in a dark pit, only rescued to be sold as a slave.
• **David** had been led to believe he would be the King of Israel, but had to flee to the wilderness as Saul tried to kill him.
• **Moses** was in the wilderness with the whole nation of Israel riding on his shoulders.
• **Elijah** hid in the desert because his words of truth angered the King.
• **Jesus** himself walked the desert places stalked by the Devil, all alone, fasting for 40 days.
• **Saul**, in his transition to becoming Paul, spent years making tents. Dreaming, hoping and learning from God.

What is the common thread here? Where is that thread of Grace that runs right through these stories like the words in a stick of rock? Could it be that these barren places of emptiness became the defining places in the history of Gods dealings with his people? A place where the burning bush was found, and the Holy Spirit falls like a dove. The place where manna falls from heaven, and rocks pour water onto thirsty ground. These desert places are full of stories of renewed vision and of redemption. Perhaps above all things however, in the wilderness we find again a longing for reliance and dependence- where confidence in our own strength slips away- stolen by the night wolves and the birds riding the heat of the day, leaving only a desperate need for shelter, for protection, and to hear the very voice of God...

It is in this place that God loves to meet with us, and the place that we finally turn to Him. No more short cuts or easy compromises. No more hiding behind the busy day.

Brothers and sisters- whatever wilderness you find yourself in, keep walking.

He will find you.

Humbled

For those unused to seeing
Blind from modern light
Beauty seeps in slowly
Like morning after night
It rises up so gently
Like tide around a pole
Giving ever freely
Many things I thought I'd stole

In sweeping arc of wipers
Framed for you and me
Out in the middle distance
All possibility
So we head on up north again
And this mystery unfolds
In wilderness all glorious
Is brokenness made whole

There's a wind across these waters
Cold but ever true
It's stirring up the things in me
I never thought I knew
There's a grace in every motion
Every ebb and flow
Such wonder in the moment
Peace inside that grows

And I'm humbled
Broken down into the very soil
Taken as the ground about me rolls
Caught between the body and the soul.

Chris Goan, Poolewe 2004

NOTES ON USE OF 40 AS A DRAMATIC PRESENTATION.

The words and images in this book were originally combined for the purposes of a presenting them as a play/mediation/dramatic reading/art installation (pick a description that suits you best- I always struggled!). The group of Christians using this material were a collection of varied individuals from different churches in Dunoon Scotland, who came together in an arts group called Aoradh (Gaelic for adoration, pronunciation debateable). Our plan was to use it in different environments- secular and sacred.

The material works well for three voices- we experimented with the phrasing, finding the natural rhythm and flow of the sentences as we read the pieces through. We had one voice that did most of the narrative bits, and another who always spoke the words of Jesus in the first person. The third voice took a second, reflective narrative, and also the voice of the devil. It is entirely possible for one person to read the whole thing, or to use two voices only. Working on the material this way helps each person reading it to inhabit the words, and to find a rhythm and pace that suits what they want to convey- or at least, I hope so!

We projected the images using a data projector into a darkened room, and gave as much space and time to the words associated to each image as felt right. It seemed to work best to advance the slides on a click rather than automatically as some slides seemed to need longer- both because of having more or less words, and differing emotional content.

If you would like sounds to accompany presentation, the music on the CD version of 40 (by musicians from Leeds based alternative worship group Revive) is great. Or you can use silence, or find a sound loop of desert wind. We also played some music during three of the slides- the three where Jesus is asleep in the cave before being visited by Satan- this gave a good transition from the journey to the place of temptation.

The presentation takes about 45 minutes, and so can be done as a stand alone piece, or as part of a larger act of worship or art.

Some other ideas we played about with (some we rejected, others we kept!)

- Projecting desert images onto the walls using slide projectors/OHPs
- Covering the floor with plastic sheets and a layer of sand (if you dare!)
- Lighting the room in a wash of low blue light- perhaps fade to red as the devil enters the scene.
- Keep the space as empty as possible if you have a choice
- Using a desert wind sound loop as people gather
- Sending people away with a pebble as a reminder- carried down from a mountain top, or fetched from a remote beach (B and Q pea gravel is also good).
- Obvious time of year to use the material is Lent, but seems to work whenever!
- Doing the presentation in a pub

If you have any better ideas, we would love to hear from you! If you want to check anything out- then likewise, feel free to contact us also.

May God bless you as you get creative- he did us!

Chris Goan

You might find these links useful:

www.aoradh.com (Chris Goan's site)
www.simonsmithillustrator.co.uk (Simons site- loads of brilliant images)
www.revive.org.uk (Music, materials, inspiration)
www.proost.co.uk   (Online shop, loads of interesting stuff)
www.alternativeworship.org (Loads of info/connections and ideas)

What next?

What next Lord?
Open me another chapter
No more settling for second best
Lets do things your way
Hereafter

Too much of me
Too many borrowed robes
Of exterior righteousness
Enough of trying and striving
Then failing.
No more reaching for gold
To grasp only straw

So what next Jesus?
What new lands fruit and flower
In this, your chaotic
Kingdom?

Where are the chains you would break?
Let me swing the hammer.
To which prison bars can I apply
Acetylene?

And whose feet are starting to feel the rhythms
Of freedom?
For there is where I want to be.

Break the chains
On me

Dunoon prayer room, 2006